Hooked on Croch

SLIPPERS™

General Information

Many of the products used in this pattern book can be purchased from local craft, fabric and variety stores, or from the Annie's Attic Needlecraft Catalog (see Customer Service information on page 19).

Contents

Elfin Slippers

DESIGN BY **RUTH BLYTHE**

SKILL LEVEL

INTERMEDIATE

FINISHED SIZES

Instructions given fit woman's 7½-inch sole *(small)*; changes for 8½-inch *(medium)* and 9½-inch sole *(large)* are in [ ].

MATERIALS

- NaturallyCaron.com Country medium (worsted) weight yarn (3 oz/185 yds/85g per ball):
  2 [2, 2] balls #0011 gilded age
- Size F/5/3.75mm crochet hook needed for size and to obtain gauge
- Tapestry needle
- 1½-inch square piece of cardboard

4 MEDIUM

GAUGE

9 sc = 2 inches; 9 sc rows = 2 inches

PATTERN NOTE

Join with slip stitch as indicated unless otherwise stated.

INSTRUCTIONS

SLIPPER

MAKE 2.

FOOT

Row 1: Ch 31, sc in 2nd ch from hook and in each ch across, turn. *(30 sc)*

Rows 2–34 [2–38, 2–42]: Working in **back lps** *(see Stitch Guide)*, ch 1, sc in each st across, turn. At end of last row, fasten off.

Fold Foot in half lengthwise. Matching sts, sew sts on row 1 tog and sew sts on last row tog.

TRIM

Rnd 1: Working in ends of rows, join with sc in either seam, sc in end of each row and in each seam around, **join** *(see Pattern Note)* in beg sc. *(70 [78, 86] sc)*

Rnd 2: Ch 1, sc in each st around, join in beg sc. Fasten off.

STRAP

Row 1: Sk first 14 [16, 18] sts on last rnd of Trim, join with sc in next st, sc in each of next 5 sts, leaving rem sts unworked, turn.

Rows 2–12: Working in back lps, ch 1, sc in each st across, turn. At end of last row, fasten off.

Sew last row to corresponding sts on opposite side of Foot.

POMPOM

Wrap yarn around cardboard 75 times, slide lps off and tie separate strand tightly around center of all lps. Cut lps and fray ends.

Sew to top of seam on front of each Foot as shown in photo. ■

Foot Snuggies

DESIGN BY **ALINE SUPLINSKAS**

SKILL LEVEL

EASY

FINISHED SIZES

Instructions given fit woman's 9-inch sole; changes for 10-inch sole and 11-inch sole are in [ ].

MATERIALS

- Red Heart Super Saver medium (worsted) weight yarn (solid: 7 oz/364 yds/198g; multi: 5 oz/244 yds/141g per skein):
  - 1 skein each #318 watercolor and #530 orchid
- Size G/6/4mm crochet hook or size needed to obtain gauge
- Tapestry needle

GAUGE

17 sc = 4 inches; 5 sc rows = 1 inch

INSTRUCTIONS

SNUGGIE

MAKE 2.

Row 1: Starting at ankle opening, with watercolor, ch 45 [47, 49], sl st in first ch to form ring, ch 17 [20, 23], sc in 2nd ch from hook *(instep)*, sc in each of next 15 [18, 21] chs, sc in each of next 45 [47, 49] chs around ankle opening, working on opposite side of starting ch on instep, sc in each of last 16 [19, 22] chs, turn. *(77 [85, 93] sc)*

Rows 2–19: Working these rows in **back lps** *(see Stitch Guide)* only, ch 1, sc in each st across, turn.

SOLE

Row 20 (WS): Fold piece in half lengthwise, working through both thicknesses and matching sts, ch 1, sl st in each of next 38 [42, 46] sts, leaving center st at fold unworked. Fasten off.

TOE

With tapestry needle and 2 strands watercolor held tog, weave through ends of rows, pull tight to gather, secure end.

ANKLE EDGING

Row 1: With WS facing, working on opposite side of starting ch on row 1 at ankle opening, join orchid with sc in first ch, [ch 1, sk next ch, sc in next ch] across, turn. *(22 [23, 24] ch sps)*

Row 2: Sl st in first ch sp, ch 4 *(counts as first tr)*, tr in same ch sp, 2 tr in each ch sp around, join with sl st in 4th ch of beg ch-4. Fasten off.

TIE

With orchid, ch 100. Fasten off. Tie knot in each end of Tie.

Starting at front, weave through ch sps of row 1 on Ankle Edging. Tie into bow. ■

Granny Square Booties

DESIGN BY
ANNIE'S CROCHET

SKILL LEVEL

INTERMEDIATE

FINISHED SIZES

Instructions given fit women's 9-inch sole *(small)*; changes for 10-inch sole *(medium)* and 11-inch sole *(large)* are in [ ].

MATERIALS

- NaturallyCaron.com Country medium (worsted) weight yarn (3 oz/185 yds/85g per ball):
  2 [3, 3] balls #0007 naturally
  1 [1, 1] ball each #0001 rose bisque, #0002 coral lipstick, #0003 soft sunshine, #0006 berry frappe and #0004 green sheen
- Size crochet hook needed for size and to obtain gauge
- Tapestry needle

GAUGE

Size G hook for 9-inch sole: 4 sc = 1 inch; 4 sc rows = 1 inch

Size G hook and 2 strands held tog: 7 sc = 2 inches; 7 sc rows = 2 inches

Size H hook for 10-inch sole: 7 sc = 2 inches; 7 sc rows = 2 inches

Size H hook and 2 strands held tog: 3 sc = 1 inch; 3 sc rows = 1 inch

Size J hook for 11-inch sole: 3 sc = 1 inch; 3 sc rows = 1 inch

Size J hook and 2 strands held tog: 5 sc = 2 inches; 5 sc rows = 2 inches

PATTERN NOTES

Join with slip stitch as indicated unless otherwise stated.

Change colors in last stitch made. Do not carry dropped color along back of work.

Use separate ball of yarn for each section of color and fasten off each color when no longer needed.

SPECIAL STITCH

Berry stitch (berry st): Insert hook in place indicated, yo, pull lp through st, you now have 2 lps hook, keep first lp on hook, working in 2nd lp only, ch 3, yo, pull through all lps on hook.

INSTRUCTIONS

BOOTIE
MAKE 2.
SIDE PATCH
MAKE 2.

Rnd 1: With soft sunshine, ch 2, 6 sc in 2nd ch from hook, **join** *(see Pattern Notes)* in beg sc. *(6 sc)*

Rnd 2: Ch 1, 2 sc in each st around, join in beg sc. Fasten off. *(12 sc)*

Rnd 3: Join rose with sc in first st, sc in same st, **berry st** *(see Special Stitch)* in next st, 2 sc in next st, **changing colors** *(see Stitch Guide and Pattern Notes)* to berry frappe in last st, 2 sc in next st, berry st in next st, 2 sc in next st, changing to coral, 2 sc in next st, berry st in next st, 2 sc in next st, changing to green, 2 sc in next st, berry st in next st, 2 sc in last st, join in beg sc. Fasten off. *(20 sts)*

Rnd 4: Join rose with sc in first st, berry st in next st, 3 sc in next st, berry st in next st,

sc in next st, changing to berry frappe, *sc in next st, berry st in next st, 3 sc in next st, berry st in next st, sc in next st*, changing to coral, rep between * once, changing to green, rep between * once, join in beg sc. Fasten off. *(28 sts)*

Rnd 5: Join rose with sc in first st, sc in each of next 2 sts, berry st in next st, sc in each of next 3 sts, changing to berry frappe, *sc in each of next 3 sts, berry st in next st, sc in each of next 3 sts*, changing to coral, rep between * once, changing to green, rep between * once, join in beg sc. Fasten off.

Rnd 6: Join naturally with sc in first st, sc in each of next 2 sts, [3 sc in next st *(corner)*, sc in next 6 sts] 3 times, 3 sc in next st *(corner)*, sc in each of last 3 sts, join in beg sc. *(36 sc)*

Rnds 7 & 8: Ch 1, sc in each st around with 3 sc in each center corner st, join in beg sc. At end of last rnd, fasten off. *(52 sc at end of last rnd)*

Row 9: Now working in rows, join naturally with sc in 3rd st of any 3-sc group, sc in each of next 11 sts leaving rem sts unworked. Fasten off.

Row 10: Sk next 14 sts on rnd 8, join naturally with sc in next st, sc in each of next 11 sts, leaving rem sts unworked. Fasten off.

HEEL

Hold Side Patches WS tog, matching sts of row 10, working through both thicknesses, join naturally with sc in first st, sc in each st across. Fasten off.

TOP PATCH

Rnds 1–4: Rep rnds 1–4 of Side Patch.

Rnd 5: Join rose with sc in first st, sc in next st, berry st in next st, sc in next st, berry st in next st, sc in each of next 2 sts, changing to berry frappe, *sc in each of next 2 sts, berry st in next st, sc in next st, berry st in next st, sc in each of next 2 sts*, changing to coral, rep between * once, changing to green, rep between * once, join in beg sc. Fasten off.

Rnd 6: Join rose with sc in first st, sc in same st, sc in each of next 2 sts, (sc, berry st, sc) in next st, sc in each of next 2 sts, 2 sc in next st, changing to berry frappe, *2 sc in next st, sc in each of next 2 sts, (sc, berry st, sc) in next st, sc in each of next 2 sts, 2 sc in next st*, changing to coral, rep between * once, changing to green, rep between * once, join in beg sc. Fasten off.

Rnd 7: Join naturally with sc in first st, 2 sc in same st, sc in each of next 4 sts, 2 sc in next st, sc in each of next 4 sts, 3 sc in next st, sc in each st around, join in beg sc. *(49 sc)*

Rnd 8: Ch 1, sc in first st, 3 sc in next st, sc in each of next 5 sts, 2 sc in each of next 2 sts, sc in each of next 5 sts, 3 sc in next st, sc in each st around, join in beg sc. *(55 sc)*

Rnd 9: Ch 1, sc in each of first 2 sts, 3 sc in next st, sc in each of next 6 sts, 2 sc in next st, sc in each of next 2 sts, 2 sc in next st, sc in each of next 6 sts, 3 sc in next st, sc in each st around, join in beg sc. *(61 sc)*

Rnd 10: Ch 1, sc in each of first 2 sts, hold sts of row 9 on 1 end of Side Patches and Top Patch WS tog, matching sts, working through both thicknesses, sc in each of next 12 sts, working through both thicknesses of sts on opposite end of Side Patches and Top Patch, sc in each of next 12 sts, sc in each st around Top Patch, join in beg sc. Fasten off.

SOLE

Rnd 1: With 2 strands naturally held tog, ch 24, 2 sc in 2nd ch from hook, sc in each of next 10 chs, hdc in next ch, dc in each of next 9 chs, 2 dc in next ch, 5 dc in last ch, working on opposite side of ch, 2 dc in next ch, dc in each of next 9 chs, hdc in next ch, sc in each of last 11 chs, join in beg sc. *(52 sts)*

Rnd 2: Ch 1, sc in first st, 2 sc in next st, sc in each of next 23 sts, 2 hdc in next st, 3 hdc in next st, 2 hdc in next st, sc in each of next 23 sts, 2 sc in last st, join in beg sc. *(58 sts)*

Rnd 3: Ch 1, sc in first st, 2 sc in next st, sc in each of next 12 sts, sk next st, sc in each of next 10 sts, [2 sc in next st, sc in each of next 3 sts] twice, 2 sc in next st, sc in each of next 10 sts, sk next st, sc in each of next 12 sts, 2 sc in last st, join in beg sc. *(61 sc)*

SMALL SIZE ONLY

Fasten off.

MEDIUM & LARGE SIZES ONLY

Rnd 4: Ch 1, sc in first st, 2 sc in next st, sc in each of next 27 sts, 2 sc in next st, sc in each of next 3 sts, 2 sc in next st, sc in each of next 26 sts, 2 sc in last st, join in beg sc. Fasten off. *(56 sc)*

With naturally, easing to fit, sc Sole to bottom of Bootie. ■

HOT Boots

DESIGN BY **DOROTHY WARRELL**

SKILL LEVEL

INTERMEDIATE

FINISHED SIZES

Instructions given fit woman's 9-inch sole *(small)*; changes for 10-inch sole *(medium)* and 11-inch sole *(large)* are in [ ].

MATERIALS

- TLC Essentials medium (worsted) weight yarn (6 oz/ 312 yds/170g per skein):
  1 [1, 1] skein #2820 robin egg
- Size H/8/5mm crochet hook or size needed to obtain gauge
- Tapestry needle
- Stitch markers

4 MEDIUM

GAUGE

7 hdc = 2 inches

PATTERN NOTES

Join with slip stitch as indicated unless otherwise stated.

Chain-3 at beginning of row or round counts as first double crochet unless otherwise stated.

INSTRUCTIONS

BOOT

MAKE 2.

SOLE

Rnd 1: Ch 26 [30, 34], hdc in 2nd ch from hook, mark this st, hdc in each ch across with 3 hdc in last ch, place marker in first and last hdc of 3-hdc group, working on opposite side of ch, hdc in each ch across with 2 hdc in last ch, mark first hdc of this group, **join** *(see Pattern Notes)* in beg hdc. *(52 [60, 68] hdc)*

Rnd 2: Ch 1, 2 hdc in first st, hdc in each st across to marker, move markers as you work, 2 hdc in each of next 3 sts, hdc in each st around to next marker, 2 hdc in each of last 2 sts, join in beg hdc. *(58 [66, 74] hdc)*

Rnd 3: Ch 1, 2 hdc in first st, hdc in each st around to next marker, [2 hdc in next st, hdc in next st] 3 times, hdc in each st around to next marker, [2 hdc in next st, hdc in next st] twice, join in beg hdc. *(64 [72, 80] hdc)*

Rnd 4: Ch 1, 2 hdc in first st, hdc in each st around to next marker, [2 hdc in next st, hdc in each of next 2 sts] 3 times, hdc in each st around to next marker, [2 hdc in next st, hdc in each of next 2 sts] twice, join in beg hdc. *(70 [78, 86] hdc)*

Rnd 5: Ch 2, **bpdc** *(see Stitch Guide)* around first st, bpdc around each st around, join in beg bpdc.

Rnd 6: Ch 2, dc in first st and in each st around, join in beg dc.

Rnd 7: Ch 1, hdc in first st, hdc in each st around to center 9 sts between markers, [**hdc dec** *(see Stitch Guide)* in next 2 sts, hdc in next st] 3 times *(toe)*, hdc in each st around, join in beg hdc. Fasten off. *(67 [75, 83] hdc)*

TOP

Row 1: Fold Boot Sole in half lengthwise to locate center back, with RS facing, ch 11, join with sc in 16th st from center back, sc in each ch across, turn. *(11 sc)*

Row 2: **Ch 3** *(see Pattern Notes)*, dc in each st across, working on inside of Boot toward back, sc in each of next 3 sts on rnd 7 of Sole, turn.

Row 3: Sk first 3 sc, sc in each dc across, turn.

Rows 4–21: [Rep rows 2 and 3 alternately] 9 times.

Row 22: Ch 3, dc in each st across, dc in same st as last sc on Sole, dc in each of next 14 [18, 22] sts, [**dc dec** *(see Stitch Guide)* in next 2 sts, dc in next st] 3 times, dc in each of next 13 [17, 21] sts, dc in same st as first sc made on row 1 of Top, working on opposite side of ch on row 1, dc in each ch across, turn. *(57 [65, 73] sts)*

Row 23: Ch 1, sc in each st across, turn.

Row 24: Ch 3, dc in each st across to center 9 sts at toe, [dc dec in next 2 sts, dc in next st] 3 times, dc in each st across, turn.

Row 25: Working through both thicknesses, sl st tog in **back lps** *(see Stitch Guide)* from top to toe to close. Fasten off.

TIE

Cut 90-inch length of yarn. Fold in half. Secure fold to solid object, twist clockwise until yarn begs to twist when tension is released. Bring ends tog and allow to twist. Tie knot in each end.

Weave Tie through openings between 3 sts of Top where it joins to Sole at Ankle.

BALL
MAKE 2.

Row 1: Cut 90-inch length of yarn, fold in half, beg at fold with both strands held tog, ch 2, 6 sc in 2nd ch from hook, turn. *(6 sc)*

Row 2: Ch 1, 2 sc in each st across, turn. *(12 sc)*

Row 3: Ch 1, [**sc dec** *(see Stitch Guide)* in next 2 sts] across. Leaving long end, fasten off. *(6 sc)*

Stuff unworked end into Ball. With long end, sew rows 1 and 3 tog. Secure end.

Attach 1 Ball to each end of Tie.

EDGING

Join in center back, ch 3, (sl st, ch 3) around, join in beg sl st. Fasten off. ■

Bedroom Booties

DESIGN BY **JOYCE LOVEJOY**

SKILL LEVEL

EASY

FINISHED SIZES

Instructions given fit woman's 9½-inch sole; changes for 10½-inch sole and 11½-inch sole are in [ ].

MATERIALS

- NaturallyCaron.com Country medium (worsted) weight yarn (3 oz/185 yds/85g per ball):
  2 [3, 3] balls #0006 berry frappe
- Size J/10/6mm crochet hook or size needed to obtain gauge
- Tapestry needle
- Stitch marker

4 MEDIUM

GAUGE

3 sc = 1 inch; 7 sc rows = 2 inches

PATTERN NOTES

Hold 2 strands of yarn together unless otherwise stated.

Work in continuous rounds, do not turn or join unless otherwise stated.

Mark first stitch of each round.

INSTRUCTIONS

BOOTIE

MAKE 2.

Rnd 1: Beg at toe, with **2 strands yarn held tog** *(see Pattern Notes)*, ch 2, 6 [7, 8], sc in 2nd ch from hook, **do not join** *(see Pattern Notes)*. *(6 [7, 8] sc)*

Rnds 2 & 3: 2 sc in each st around. *(24 [28, 32] sc at end of last rnd)*

Rnds 4–14 [4–16, 4–18]: Sc in each st around. At end of last rnd, join with sl st in beg sc.

SIDES & HEEL

Row 15 [17, 19]: Now working in rows, ch 7, sc in 2nd ch from hook, [ch 1, sk next ch, sc in next ch] twice, ch 1, sk next ch, sc in same st as joining sl st on last rnd, [ch 1, sk next st, sc in next st] 11 [13, 15] times, ch 1, sk next st, sc in sl st, working on opposite side of chs, [ch 1, sk next ch, sc in next ch] 3 times, turn. *(19 [21, 23] sc)*

Rows 16–33 [18–37, 20–40]: Ch 1, sc in first st, [ch 1, sk next ch sp, sc in next st] across, turn. At end of last row, fasten off.

With RS tog, fold last row in half, sew back seam.

FLOWER

MAKE 2.

Rnd 1: With 1 strand of yarn, ch 3, sl st in first ch to form ring, ch 3 *(counts as first dc)*, 20 dc in ring, join with sl st in 3rd ch of beg ch-3. *(21 dc)*

Rnd 2: Ch 3, 4 dc in same st, 5 dc in each st around, join with sl st in 3rd ch of beg ch-3. Fasten off. *(105 dc)*

Sew Flower to center front of Bootie as shown in photo. ■

Tweed Rolltop Slippers

DESIGN BY **DOROTHY WARRELL**

SKILL LEVEL

INTERMEDIATE

FINISHED SIZES

Instructions given fit woman's 9-inch sole *(small)*; changes for 9½-inch sole *(medium)* and 10-inch sole *(large)* are in [ ].

MATERIALS

- Red Heart Super Saver medium (worsted) weight yarn (7 oz/ 364 yds/198g per skein):
  1 [1, 1] skein each #374 country rose and #313 aran
- Size H/8/5mm afghan crochet hook or size needed to obtain gauge
- Tapestry needle
- Stitch markers

GAUGE

4 pattern sts = 1 inch; 3 pattern rows = 1 inch

SPECIAL STITCHES

Work lps off hook: Yo, pull through 1 lp on hook *(see A of Fig. 1)*, [yo, pull through 2 lps on hook] across leaving 1 lp on hook at end of row *(see B of Fig. 1)*.

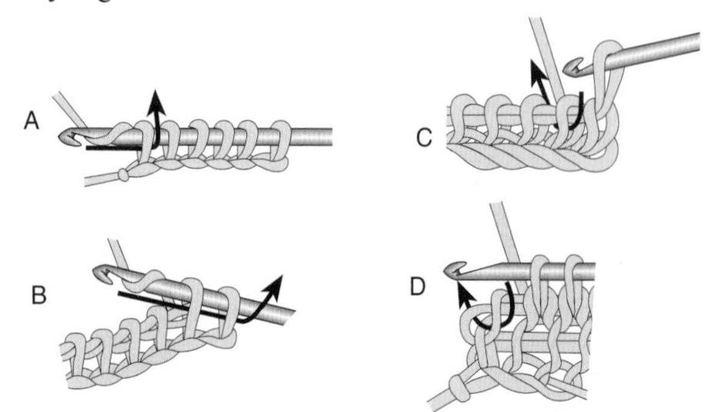

Fig. 1
Afghan Stitch

Afghan stitch (afghan st): Sk first vertical bar, pull up lp in next vertical bar *(see C of Fig. 1)*, pull up lp in each vertical bar across to last vertical bar, for last st, insert hook in last bar and st directly behind it *(see D of Fig. 1)* at same time, yo, pull lp through, work lps off hook.

Knit stitch (knit st): With yarn in back, insert hook from front to back *(see Fig. 2)*.

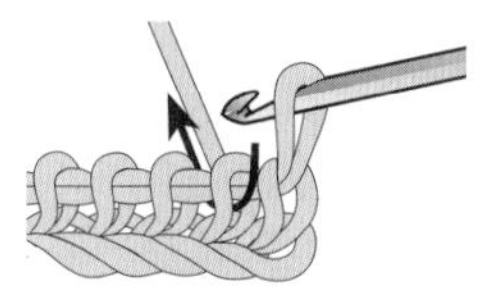

Fig. 2
Afghan Knit Stitch

Purl stitch (purl st): With yarn in front, insert hook around back bar *(see Fig. 3)*.

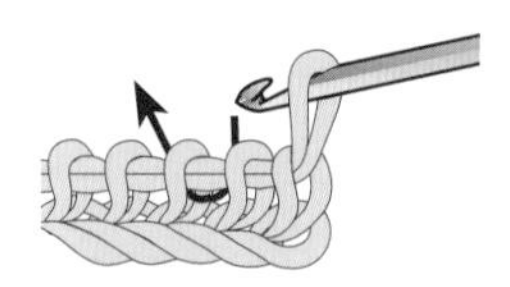

Fig. 3
Afghan Purl Stitch

INSTRUCTIONS

SLIPPER

MAKE 2.

Row 1: With rose, ch 26, pull up lp in 2nd ch from hook and in each ch across, drop rose, pick up aran, **work lps off hook** *(see Special Stitches)*.

Row 2: ***Purl st** *(see Special Stitches)* in next st**, **knit st** *(see Special Stitches)* in next st, rep from * across, ending last rep at **, work **last st** *(see D of Fig. 1)*, drop aran, with rose, work lps off hook.

Row 3: *Knit st in next st**, purl in next st, rep from * across, ending last rep at **, work last st, with aran, work lps off hook.

Rows 4–26 [4–28, 4–30]: [Rep rows 2 and 3 alternately] 12 [13, 14] times, ending last rep with row 2. At end of last row, fasten off aran.

Last row: *Knit st in next st**, purl in next st, rep from * across, ending last rep at **, work last st, yo, pull through 1 lp, [yo, pull through 4 lps] across, yo, pull through last lp. Leaving long end, fasten off.

CUFF

Row 1: With RS facing and working in ends of rows, with rose, pull up lps in each row across, pull up lp in ch on opposite side of row 1 *(28 [30, 32] lps on hook)*, work off lps.

Rows 2–5: Knit st across, work off lps. At end of last row, fasten off.

Rep Cuff on opposite edge.

FINISHING

Fold piece in half lengthwise, with RS facing, sew back seam including Cuff.

Turn up point at heel, flatten point across seam and sew in place.

With long end, sew toe tog and bottom row of Cuff for 3½ [4, 4] inches.

Roll Cuff to RS, sl st last row of Cuff to first row. Fasten off. ■

Foliage Slippers

DESIGN BY **DARLA SIMS**

SKILL LEVEL

EASY

FINISHED SIZES

Instructions given fit woman's 8-inch sole; changes for 8½-inch sole, 9½-inch sole and 10½-inch sole are in [ ].

MATERIALS

- NaturallyCaron.com Country medium (worsted) weight yarn (3 oz/185 yds/85g per ball):
  2 [3, 3] balls #0012 foliage
- Size H/8/5mm crochet hook or size needed to obtain gauge
- Tapestry needle

4 MEDIUM

GAUGE

7 hdc = 2 inches; 13 hdc rows = 5 inches

PATTERN NOTES

Chain-2 at beginning of row or round counts as first half double crochet unless otherwise stated.

Join with slip stitch as indicated unless otherwise stated.

SPECIAL STITCHES

Half double crochet popcorn (hdc pc): 5 hdc in place indicated, drop lp from hook, insert in first st of hdc group, pull dropped lp through st.

Single crochet popcorn (sc pc): 5 sc in place indicated, drop lp from hook, insert in first st of sc group, pull dropped lp through st.

INSTRUCTIONS

SLIPPER

MAKE 2.

Row 1: Ch 33, hdc in 3rd ch from hook *(first 2 chs count as first hdc)*, hdc in each ch across, turn. *(32 hdc)*

Rows 2–16 [2–18, 2–20, 2–22]: **Ch 2** *(see Pattern Notes)*, hdc in each st across, turn.

Row 17 [19, 21, 23]: Ch 2, [hdc in each of next 3 sts, **hdc dec** *(see Stitch Guide)* in next 2 sts] across, turn. *(26 hdc)*

Row 18 [20, 22, 24]: Ch 2, hdc in each st across, turn.

Row 19 [21, 23, 25]: Ch 2, [hdc in each of next 3 sts, hdc dec in next 2 sts] across, turn. *(21 hdc)*

Row 20 [22, 24, 26]: Ch 2, hdc in each st across, turn.

Row 21 [23, 25, 27]: Ch 2, [hdc dec in next 2 sts] across. Fasten off.

Fold Slipper in half, sew starting ch on row 1 tog.

Sew ends of rows 17–21 [17–23, 17–25, 17–27] on instep tog. Gather and sew toe closed.

CUFF

Rnd 1: Working in ends of rows around ankle opening, join with sc in row before seam at heel, evenly sp 17 sc across side of ankle opening, evenly sp 18 sc across rem side, **join** *(see Pattern Notes)* in beg sc. *(36 sc)*

Rnd 2: Ch 2, hdc in each st around, join in 2nd ch of beg ch-2.

Rnd 3: Ch 2, **fptr** *(see Stitch Guide)* around next st on row before last, sk st on this row behind fptr, *hdc in each of next 2 sts, sk next 4 sts from last fptr on row before last, fptr around next st, sk st on this row behind fptr, [hdc in each of next 2 sts, fptr around next st on row before last, sk st on this row behind fptr] twice**, hdc in each of next 2 sts, sk next 4 sts from last fptr on row before last, fptr around next st, sk st on this row behind fptr, rep from * around, ending last rep at **, hdc in last st, join in 2nd ch of beg ch-2.

Rnd 4: Ch 2, hdc in each st around, join in 2nd ch of beg ch-2.

Rnd 5: Ch 2, *fptr around next fptr below, hdc in each of next 5 sts, **hdc pc** *(see Special Stitches)* in next fptr, sk st on this row behind hdc pc**, hdc in each of next 5 sts, rep from * around, ending last rep at **, hdc in each of last 4 sts, join in 2nd ch of beg ch-2.

Rnd 6: Ch 2, hdc in each st around, join in 2nd ch of beg ch-2.

Rnd 7: Ch 1, sc in each of first 2 sts, **sc pc** *(see Special Stitches)* in next st, [sc in each of next 2 sts, sc pc in next st] around, join in beg sc.

Rnd 8: Ch 1, sc in each st around, join in beg sc. Fasten off. ■

LOAFERS

DESIGN BY **DARLA SIMS**

SKILL LEVEL

INTERMEDIATE

FINISHED SIZES

Instructions given fit 8½-inch sole; changes for 9-inch sole, 9½-inch sole and 10½-inch sole are in [ ].

MATERIALS

- NaturallyCaron.com Country medium (worsted) weight yarn (3 oz/185 yds/85g per ball: 2 [2, 2, 3] balls #0021 peacock

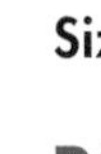

- Size H/8/5mm and I/9/5.5mm crochet hooks or sizes needed to obtain gauge

GAUGE

Size H hook: 7 sc = 2 inches

Size I hook: 3 sts = 1 inch; 7 sc rnds = 2 inches

PATTERN NOTES

Use size I hook and 2 strands of yarn held together unless otherwise stated.

Join with slip stitch as indicated unless otherwise stated.

INSTRUCTIONS

LOAFER

MAKE 2.

FOOT

Rnd 1: Beg at heel with 2 strands held tog *(see Pattern Notes)*, ch 18, [20, 22, 24], sc in 2nd ch from hook, sc in each ch across to last ch, 3 sc in last ch, working on opposite side of chs, sc in each ch across to last ch, 2 sc in last ch, **join** *(see Pattern Notes)* in beg sc. *(36 [40, 44, 48] sc)*

Rnd 2: Ch 1, 2 sc in first st, sc in each of next 10 [12, 14, 16] sts, hdc in each of next 3 sts, dc in each of next 2 sts, 2 dc in each of next 4 sts, dc in each of next 2 sts *(toe)*, hdc in each of next 3 sts, sc in each of next 10 [12, 14, 16] sts, 2 sc in last st, join in beg sc. *(42 [46, 50, 54] sts)*

Rnd 3: Ch 1, 2 sc in first st, sc in each of next 11 [13, 15, 17] sts, hdc in each of next 3 sts, dc in each of next 2 sts, 2 dc in each of next 6 sts, dc in each of next 2 sts, hdc in each of next 3 sts, sc in each of next 11 [13, 15, 17] sts, 2 sc in each of last 3 sts, join in beg sc. *(52 [56, 60, 64] sts)*

Rnd 4: Ch 1, 2 sc in each of first 3 sts, sc in each of next 20 [22, 24, 26] sts, 2 sc in each of next 6 sts, sc in each of next 20 [22, 24, 26] sts, 2 sc in each of last 3 sts, join in beg sc. *(64 [68, 72, 76] sc)*

Rnd 5: Working this rnd in **back lps** *(see Stitch Guide)* only, ch 1, sc in each st around, join in beg sc.

Rnds 6–8: Ch 1, sc in each st around, join in beg sc. At end of last rnd, fasten off.

INSTEP

Rnd 1: Ch 8, sc in 2nd ch from hook, sc in each of next 5 chs, 3 sc in last ch, working on opposite side of chs, sc in each of next 5 chs, 2 sc in last ch, join in beg sc. *(16 sc)*

Rnd 2: Ch 1, 2 sc in first st, sc in each of next 5 sts, 2 sc in each of next 3 sts, sc in each of next 5 sts, 2 sc in each of last 2 sts, join in beg sc. *(22 sc)*

Rnd 3: Ch 1, sc in each of first 8 sts, 2 sc in each of next 3 sts, sc in each of next 8 sts, 2 sc in each of last 3 sts, join in beg sc. *(28 sc)*

Rnd 4: Ch 1, sc in each of first 11 sts, 2 sc in each of next 3 sts, sc in each of next 11 sts, 2 sc in each of last 3 sts, join in beg sc. Fasten off. *(34 sc)*

JOINING

Rnd 1: Matching sts on Instep to center 28 sts on toe, with size I hook, working in back lps through both thicknesses, join in first st on Instep and first st of center 28 sts on Foot, sl st in each of next 27 sts, with size H hook, working in both lps of Foot only, [sc in each of next 3 sts, **sc dec** *(see Stitch Guide)* in next 2 sts] 7 [8, 8, 9] times, for sizes 8½ inches, 9½ inches and 10½ inches only, sc in each of last 1 [4, 3] sts, **for all sizes**, join in next st on Instep, **turn.**

Row 2: Ch 1, sc in each st across, sl st in next st on Instep. Fasten off. ■

Bed Socks

DESIGN BY **LINDA GUERIN**

SKILL LEVEL

INTERMEDIATE

FINISHED SIZE

One size fits most adults

MATERIALS

- NaturallyCaron.com Country medium (worsted) weight yarn (3 oz/185 yds/85g per ball):
  2 balls each #0007 naturally and #0017 claret
- Size H/8/5mm crochet hook or size needed to obtain gauge
- Tapestry needle
- Stitch marker

GAUGE

7 sc = 2 inches; 7 sc rows = 2 inches

PATTERN NOTES

Work in continuous rounds, do not join or turn unless otherwise stated.

Mark first stitch of each round.

SPECIAL STITCHES

Single crochet foundation (sc foundation): Ch 2, insert hook in 2nd ch from hook, yo, pull lp through, yo, pull through 1 lp on hook *(ch-1 completed)*, yo, pull through all lps on hook *(sc completed)*, [insert hook in last ch-1, yo, pull lp through, yo, pull through 1 lp on hook *(ch-1 completed)*, yo, pull through both lps on hook *(sc completed)*] as stated in instructions.

Slip ring: Leaving 4-inch end on thread, lap thread over 4-inch end forming lp, insert hook through lp from front to back, yo *(Fig. 1)*, pull through lp to form ring, yo, pull through lp on hook.

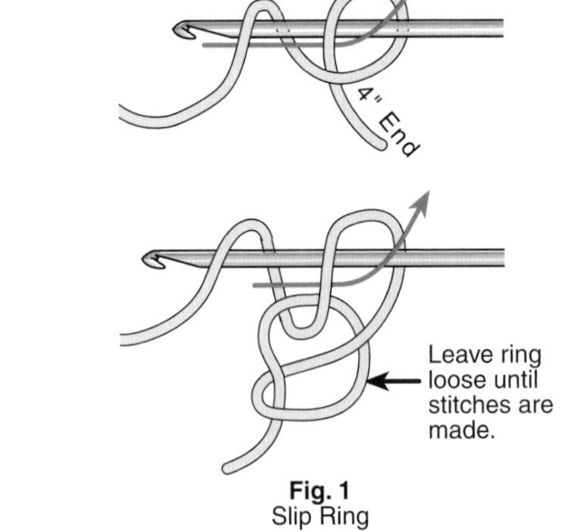

Fig. 1
Slip Ring

INSTRUCTIONS

SOCK

MAKE 2.

TOP

Row 1: With naturally, work 12 **sc foundation** *(see Special Stitches)*, turn. *(12 sc)*

Rows 2–46: Working in **back lps** *(see Stitch Guide)*, ch 1, sc in each st across, turn. At end of last row, fasten off.

BOTTOM

Row 1: With claret, work 48 sc foundation, turn. *(48 sc)*

Rows 2–21: Ch 1, sc in each st across, turn. At end of last row, fasten off.

TOE

Rnd 1: With naturally, make **slip ring** *(see Special Stitches)*, 6 sc in ring, **do not join** *(see Pattern Notes)*, pull end to close ring.

Rnd 2: 2 sc in each st around. *(12 sc)*

Rnd 3: [Sc in next st, 2 sc in next st] around. *(18 sc)*

Rnd 4: Sc in each st around.

Rnds 5 & 6: [Sc in each of next 2 sts, 2 sc in next st] around. *(32 sc at end of last rnd)*

Rnd 7: 2 sc in first st, [sc in each of next 10 sts, 2 sc in next st] twice, sc in each of last 9 sts. *(35 sc)*

Rnd 8: Sc in each st around, join with sl st in beg sc. Fasten off.

ASSEMBLY

Easing to fit, sew or sl st long edges of Top to Bottom, forming tube.

Sew or sl st Toe to 1 end of tube.

TIE

With claret, ch 300. Fasten off.

Beg at Toe, weave 1 Tie through each Sock as shown in photo. ■

Cuffed Slippers

DESIGN BY
MARIE GREGO

SKILL LEVEL

INTERMEDIATE

FINISHED SIZES

Instructions given fit 5½-inch sole *(X-small)*; changes for 6¾-inch sole *(small)*, 8-inch sole *(medium)* and 9¾-inch sole *(large)* are in [ ].

MATERIALS

- NaturallyCaron.com Country medium (worsted) weight yarn (3 oz/185 yds/85g per ball):
  3 [3, 3, 3] balls #0002 coral lipstick
- Size G/6/4mm crochet hook needed for size and to obtain gauge
- Tapestry needle
- 3 x 6-inch piece of cardboard

GAUGE

3 sc = 1 inch

PATTERN NOTES

Try using several different scrap colors for a bright, delightful pair of Slippers.

Join with slip stitch as indicated unless otherwise stated.

INSTRUCTIONS

SLIPPER

MAKE 2.

Rnd 1: Ch 20 [27, 34, 41], 3 sc in 2nd ch from hook, sc in each ch across to last ch, 3 sc in last ch, working on opposite side of ch, sc in each c h across, **join** *(see Pattern Notes)* in beg sc. *(40 [54, 68, 82] sc)*

Rnd 2: Ch 1, sc in first sc, tr in next sc, [sc in next sc, tr in next sc] around, join in beg sc.

Rnd 3: Ch 1, tr in first sc, sc in next tr, [tr in next sc, sc in next tr] around, join in beg tr.

Rnd 4: Ch 1, sc in first sc, tr in next sc, [sc in next tr, tr in next sc] around, join in beg sc.

Rnds 5–10 [5–12, 5–12, 5–12]: [Rep rnds 3 and 4 alternately] 3 [4, 4, 4] times. At the end of last rnd, leaving long end, fasten off.

Fold Slipper opening flat across. Sew across opening to center.

CUFF

Row 1: Ch 11, sc in 2nd ch from hook, sc in each ch across, turn. *(10 sc)*

Row 2: Working in **back lps** *(see Stitch Guide)*, ch 1, sc in each of next 9 sts, sc in both lps of last sc, turn.

Row 3: Working in both lps, ch 1, sc in first sc, working in back lps, sc in each of last 9 sc, turn.

Next rows: Rep rows 2 and 3 alternately until Cuff is long enough to fit around Slipper opening, beg at center front, ending in same area as beg.

Next row: Beg at center front of opening, holding long edge of Cuff on inside of Slipper at opening and working through both thicknesses, sc Cuff to opening of Slipper, turn.

Last row: Ch 1, evenly sp sc around entire outer edge of Cuff. Fasten off.

Fold Cuff to outer edge of Slipper.

POMPOM

From cardboard, cut 2 circles, each 2½ inches in diameter. Cut ¾-inch circle from center of each cardboard circle. Holding circles tog, wrap yarn over cardboard circles until filled with yarn. Carefully insert scissors between layers of cardboard, cut strands of yarn around outer edge of circles, place a doubled length of yarn between circles, pull tightly and knot to secure. Remove cardboard circles, fluff Pompom and trim edges as desired.

Attach Pompom to center top of Slipper as shown in photo. ■

TOLL-FREE ORDER LINE or to request a free catalog (800) LV-ANNIE (800) 582-6643
Customer Service (800) AT-ANNIE (800) 282-6643, **Fax** (800) 882-6643
Visit anniesattic.com

ISBN: 978-1-59635-226-1

Printed in USA

2 3 4 5 6 7 8 9

Stitch Guide

For more complete information, visit **FreePatterns.com**

ABBREVIATIONS

beg	begin/begins/beginning
bpdc	back post double crochet
bpsc	back post single crochet
bptr	back post treble crochet
CC	contrasting color
ch(s)	chain(s)
ch-	refers to chain or space previously made (i.e. ch-1 space)
ch sp(s)	chain space(s)
cl(s)	cluster(s)
cm	centimeter(s)
dc	double crochet (singular/plural)
dc dec	double crochet 2 or more stitches together, as indicated
dec	decrease/decreases/decreasing
dtr	double treble crochet
ext	extended
fpdc	front post double crochet
fpsc	front post single crochet
fptr	front post treble crochet
g	gram(s)
hdc	half double crochet
hdc dec	half double crochet 2 or more stitches together, as indicated
inc	increase/increases/increasing
lp(s)	loop(s)
MC	main color
mm	millimeter(s)
oz	ounce(s)
pc	popcorn(s)
rem	remain/remains/remaining
rep(s)	repeat(s)
rnd(s)	round(s)
RS	right side
sc	single crochet (singular/plural)
sc dec	single crochet 2 or more stitches together, as indicated
sk	skip/skipped/skipping
sl st(s)	slip stitch(es)
sp(s)	space(s)/spaced
st(s)	stitch(es)
tog	together
tr	treble crochet
trtr	triple treble
WS	wrong side
yd(s)	yard(s)
yo	yarn over

Chain—ch: Yo, pull through lp on hook.

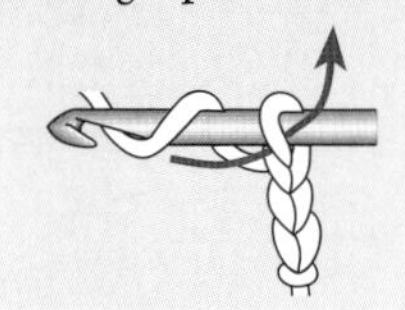

Slip stitch—sl st: Insert hook in st, pull through both lps on hook.

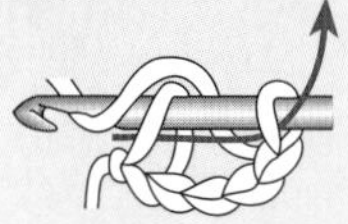

Single crochet—sc: Insert hook in st, yo, pull through st, yo, pull through both lps on hook.

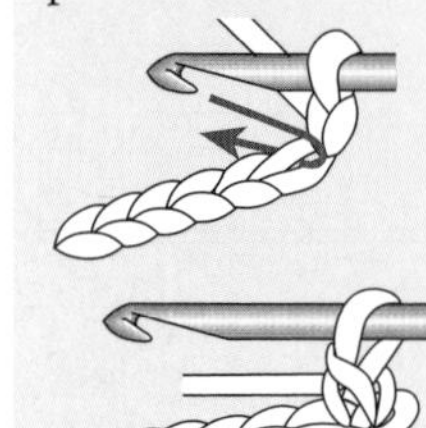

Front post stitch—fp: **Back post stitch—bp:** When working post st, insert hook from right to left around post st on previous row.

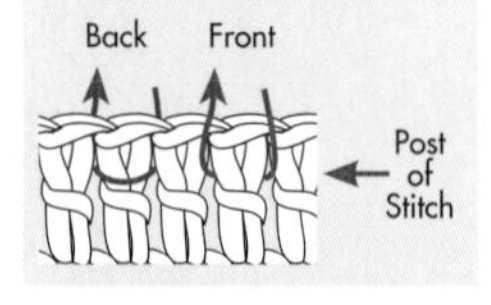

Front loop—front lp **Back loop—back lp**

Front Loop Back Loop

Half double crochet—hdc: Yo, insert hook in st, yo, pull through st, yo, pull through all 3 lps on hook.

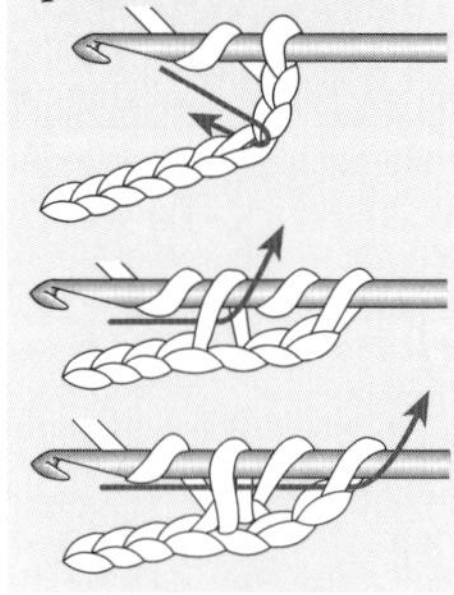

Double crochet—dc: Yo, insert hook in st, yo, pull through st, [yo, pull through 2 lps] twice.

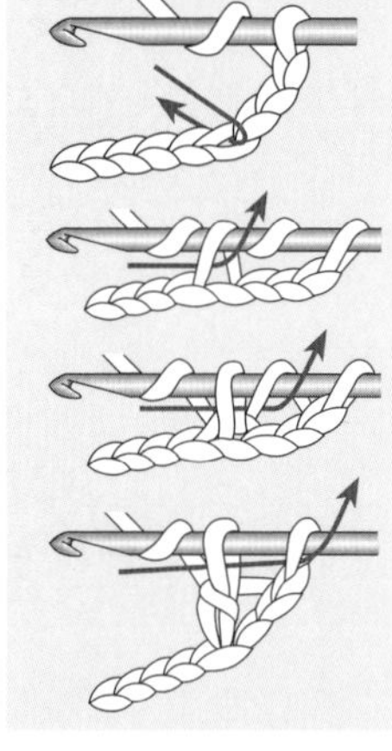

Change colors: Drop first color; with 2nd color, pull through last 2 lps of st.

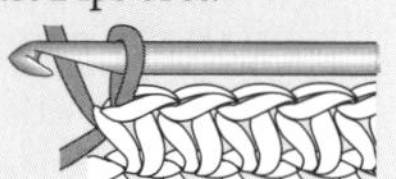

Treble crochet—tr: Yo twice, insert hook in st, yo, pull through st, [yo, pull through 2 lps] 3 times.

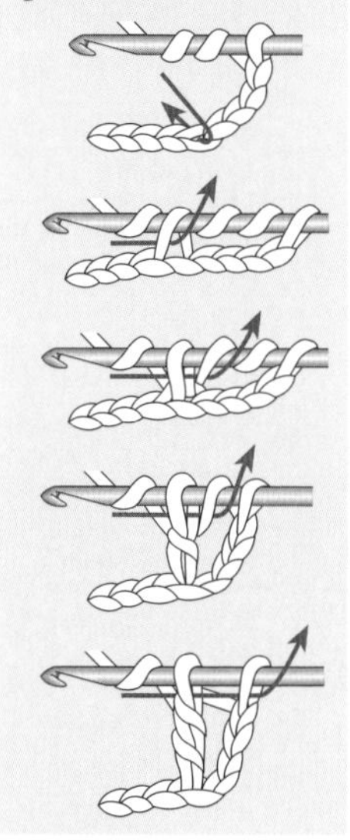

Double treble crochet—dtr: Yo 3 times, insert hook in st, yo, pull through st, [yo, pull through 2 lps] 4 times.

Single crochet decrease (sc dec): (Insert hook, yo, draw lp through) in each of the sts indicated, yo, draw through all lps on hook.

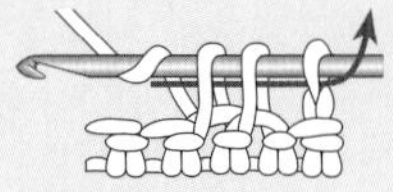

Example of 2-sc dec

Half double crochet decrease (hdc dec): (Yo, insert hook, yo, draw lp through) in each of the sts indicated, yo, draw through all lps on hook.

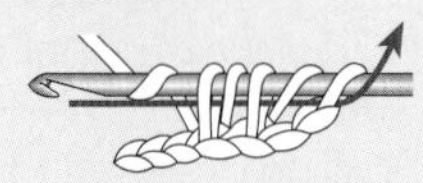

Example of 2-hdc dec

Double crochet decrease (dc dec): (Yo, insert hook, yo, draw loop through, draw through 2 lps on hook) in each of the sts indicated, yo, draw through all lps on hook.

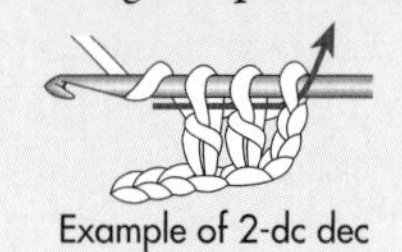

Example of 2-dc dec

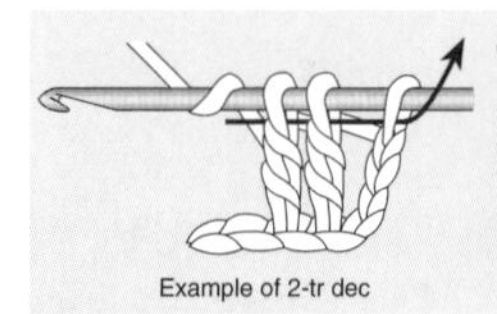

Example of 2-tr dec

Treble crochet decrease (tr dec): Holding back last lp of each st, tr in each of the sts indicated, yo, pull through all lps on hook.

US		UK
sl st (slip stitch)	=	sc (single crochet)
sc (single crochet)	=	dc (double crochet)
hdc (half double crochet)	=	htr (half treble crochet)
dc (double crochet)	=	tr (treble crochet)
tr (treble crochet)	=	dtr (double treble crochet)
dtr (double treble crochet)	=	ttr (triple treble crochet)
skip	=	miss